David's First Day at School

NIGEL SNELL

Hamish Hamilton · London

Mummy woke David very early.
It was his first day at school.
He washed and cleaned his teeth,
put on his new trousers
and went down to breakfast.

When he had finished breakfast,
Mummy said it was time to go.
He said goodbye to Oscar his pet snake,
put on his coat
and got into the car.

When they got to the school
a nice teacher was there to meet them.
She took David's hand and
he waved goodbye to Mummy.

He was a little frightened
and a big tear rolled down his cheek.
But he tried hard not to cry.

The teacher took David into a room full of other boys and girls.
She showed him his peg and helped him hang up his coat.
There was a picture of an apple near David's peg to help him remember which one was his.

Then all the children went into a big room and sat down on the floor. A lady read them a story and they sang a song.

The little girl next to David
was very friendly!

A
b
d
k
f
s
i

After that, the teacher took them to their classroom. She showed them the letters of the alphabet.

David liked the 'S' best – it reminded him of Oscar his snake.

Then a loud bell went 'ting a ling a ling' and all the boys and girls ran out to play. Another teacher was there to make sure they didn't hurt themselves.

David met some new friends
and had great fun.

Soon it was time for lessons again.
This time they had to learn
their numbers.
David made a face out of the '0'.

7
2
4
8
9

Then the bell rang again
and David and all the other
children went for their dinner.

They queued up at a little hatch
and two nice dinner ladies
gave them some food.

David had meat, red
carrots and potatoes
and pink jelly for pudding.

WRIGGLE
BOUNCE
BOUNCE
WRIGGLE

In the afternoon they all
went back into the big room.
They had to pretend to be animals.
They jumped like kangaroos,
waved their arms like birds
and wriggled on the floor like snakes.

The teacher said David was very
good at being a snake.

It was soon time to go home.
David ran out to Mummy who was waiting for him at the gate.

'It was fun', he said.
'Tomorrow we have to bring something interesting to show teacher.'

Next day David couldn't wait to get to school. He took Oscar to show to his teacher . . .

. . . but I don't think she liked him very much!

Hardback edition first published in Great Britain 1981 by
Hamish Hamilton Children's Books
Garden House, 57-59 Long Acre, London WC2E 9JZ

Reprinted 1983

Paperback edition first published 1984

British Library Cataloguing in Publication Data
Snell, Nigel
David's first day at school
I. Title
823'.914[J]   PZ7
ISBN 0-241-10641-9 (hardback)
ISBN 0-241-11195-1 (paperback)